Let's Make
Clothespin Dolls

Text & Designs Created by
Raffaella Dowling & Jessica Dowling
Photographs by
F. William Lagaret

MUD PUDDLE BOOKS
New York

Let's Make Clothespin Dolls
Text and Designs Created by
Raffaella Dowling & Jessica Dowling
Photographs by F. William Lagaret

© 2008 by Mud Puddle Books, Inc.

Published by
Mud Puddle Books, Inc.
54 W. 21st Street
Suite 601
New York, NY 10010
info@mudpuddlebooks.com

ISBN: 978-1-60311-140-9

Printed in China

Contents

Introduction

In the days before department stores and mass merchandisers were readily accessible, children used their imaginations to devise entertaining games and toys. Children then as now proved to be creative and resourceful. The making of clothespin dolls was one such invention that remains as much fun today as before. Using scraps of fabric, paper and ribbon, children were able to transform ordinary clothespins into extraordinary dolls.

The materials you need to make clothespin dolls are easy to find. They're more than likely around your house right now. In a world where most toys need batteries to operate, what better way to tap into your own creativity than to take part in a wonderful pastime like making clothespin dolls.

The Basics

To make clothespin dolls, simply use scissors and glue to transform scraps of material into tiny bits of clothing. The ease in making clothes for these dolls is that they do not need elaborate hems or joints like clothes for people. You can simply configure scraps in a way that you like to create outfits for your dolls, using glue to hold them in place.

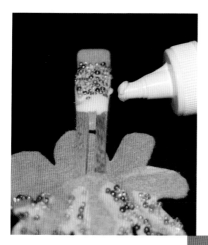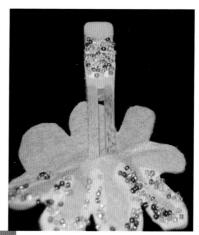

Suggested Materials

Keep in mind that you don't need to use all of these. You can also come up with other creative things to use. Look around. You're sure to be inspired.

- Plain Clothespins
- Markers
- Gel Pens
- Fabric Paints (Puffy Paint)
- Glitter
- Felt or other scrap fabric
- Colored Paper

- Sequins
- Seed Beads
- Ribbon
- Yarn
- Stickers
- Glue

Tips

Creating Faces:

You can draw a face direct-
ly on your clothespin doll
or draw a face on a small
round binder sticker and
stick it on your doll.

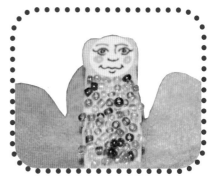

Making Yarn Hair:

To make yarn hair, make a *peace sign* (*V-sign* with your
middle and index fingers) and loop yarn several times
around your two fingers. In the middle of this yarn, tightly
tie a smaller piece of yarn. Then, cut the ends of the
loops. You now have a yarn "wig" that you can glue to
your clothespin doll's head. Experiment with different
yarn lengths and colors until you give your doll the per-
fect head of hair!

Yarn Wrapping:

Wrap yarn around the clothespin to create dresses, shirts or pants. This technique makes a great clothing base to later decorate with glitter or sequins.

Making Paper Clothes:

Make a pencil outline of a clothespin on colored paper. Using this as a template, create a paper outfit that will fit your doll. Decorate with glitter, sequins, markers— anything you like! When you are done, carefully cut out the outfit and glue it to your doll.

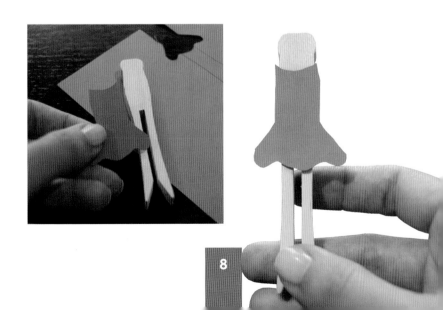

Making Fabric Clothing:

An easy way to make a dress is to wrap a rectangular piece of fabric around your clothespin doll. Add a yarn "belt" to tie it in place and proceed to decorate. You'll have a sophisticated strapless dress in no time, with no glue!

Adding Fancy Fringe:

To create a sophisticated fringe on the hem of a doll's dress or skirt, cut small slits in the bottom of the paper/fabric and gently separate.

Remember:
To prevent a sticky mess, be patient and wait for glue to dry before adding another "layer" of clothing or before decorating fabric or paper you have glued on. You won't have to wait long because ordinary glue takes no time to dry.

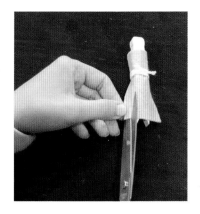
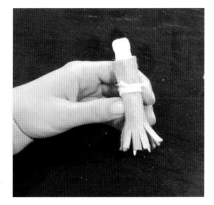

Making Arms:

To create simple arms for your clothespin doll, cut two small lengths of yarn. Tie a knot at the end of each one to make "hands." Now, trim the length of yarn so the arms are proportionate to your doll. Simply glue the yarn pieces to either side of the doll's torso.

Making Shoes:

To make simple shoes, you can cut a small piece of ribbon at a 45 degree angle for each shoe and glue it to the foot of your clothespin doll. Alternately, you can draw the shoes on with marker. For fun "slippers," try gluing a brightly colored mini pom-pom to each foot!

Since you'll have many tiny pieces of fabric, yarn and paper after making these dolls, it's a good idea to keep a special box for them (an empty shoe box with a lid would be fine). Fill this box with the materials you need so you will always have them at hand when you want to make clothespin dolls. The box will keep the scraps organized, and they won't clutter up your house!

Ways to use clothespin dolls:

- Make into Christmas ornaments.

- Make sports-themed dolls and give one to each player on your team.

- Decorate an empty shoebox with markers and glitter, and use it as a dollhouse for your clothespin dolls.

- Make a clothespin doll to represent each member of your family.

- Make clothespin dolls of your pets.

Most of all, have fun!

Sporty Fun!

Splashy

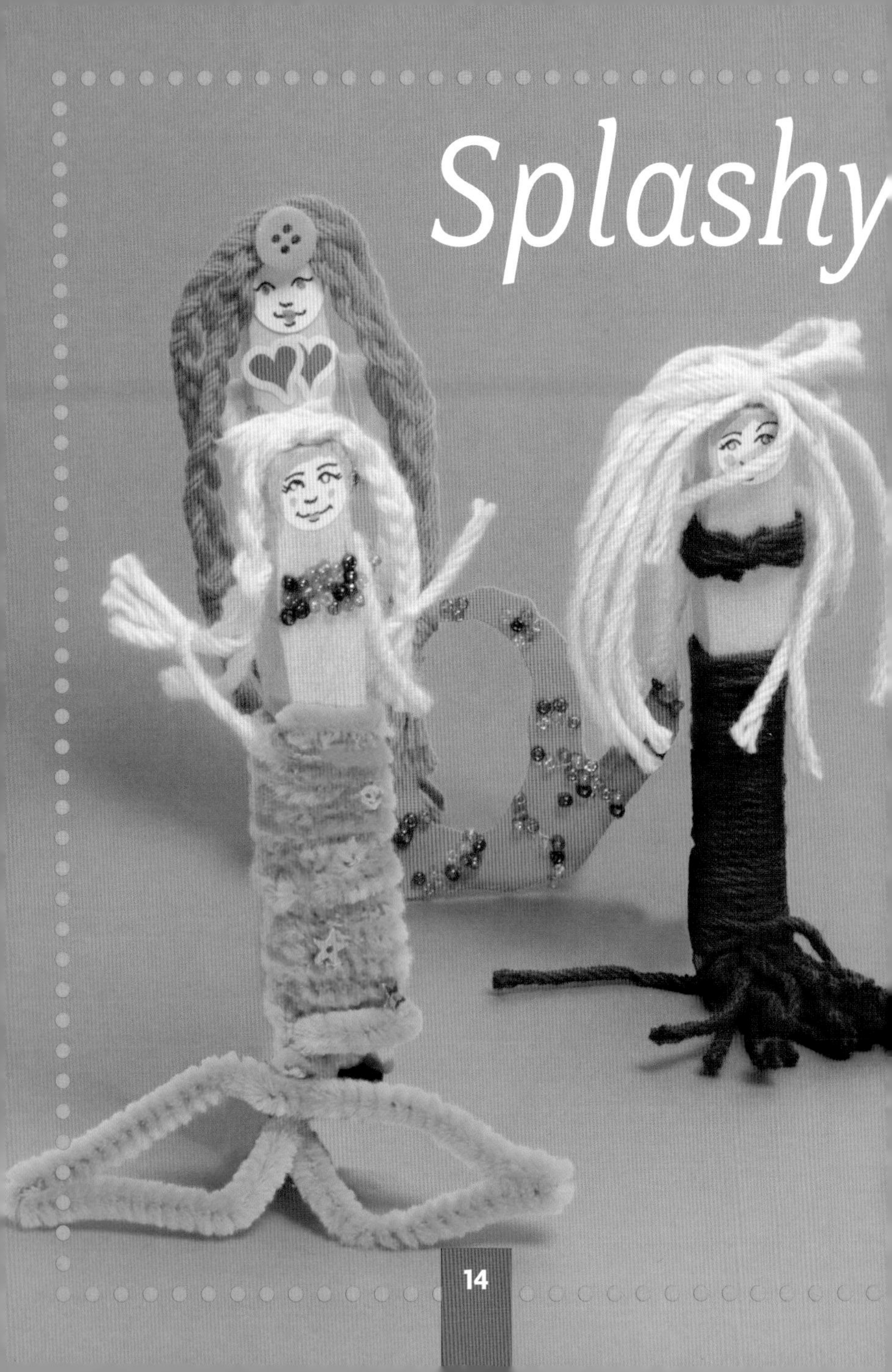

Mermaids

Princess

Pageant!

Cool Careers

Fantasy

Fairies!

Flower Power!

Beauties!

Feathered

Friends

Groovy Gals!

Christmas

Cuties!